GUARDING
AIR FORCE ONE

BY BRANDON TERRELL

Published by The Child's World®
1980 Lookout Drive • Mankato, MN 56003-1705
800-599-READ • www.childsworld.com

Acknowledgments
The Child's World®: Mary Swensen, Publishing Director
Red Line Editorial: Editorial direction and production
The Design Lab: Design

Design Element: Iaroslav Neliubov/Shutterstock Images
Photographs ©: Mic Smith/AP Images, cover, 1; Shutterstock Images,
5; Cliff Owen/AP Images, 7; AP Images, 9; Museum of Flight/Corbis, 10;
Michael Reynolds/epa/Corbis, 12; Eric Draper/White House/AP Images,
15; Pete Souza/White House, 17; Jacquelyn Martin/AP Images, 18;
Airman 1st Class Erin O'Shea/U.S. Air Force photo, 21

ISBN 9781503808089
LCCN 2015958279

Printed in the United States of America
Mankato, MN
June, 2016
PA02302

ABOUT THE AUTHOR

Brandon Terrell is a Saint Paul-based writer
of numerous children's books, including
picture books, chapter books, and graphic
novels. When not hunched over his laptop,
Brandon enjoys watching movies and
television, reading, playing baseball, and
spending every spare moment with his wife
and their two children.

TABLE OF CONTENTS

CHAPTER 1

The President's Plane 4

CHAPTER 2

From Horses to Planes 8

CHAPTER 3

Inside the Flying Fortress ...14

CHAPTER 4

Flying into the Future.......20

GLOSSARY. 22

TO LEARN MORE 23

INDEX 24

The President's Plane

A lone airplane cuts across the sky. It comes in for a landing. The plane is blue and white. UNITED STATES OF AMERICA is on the side. There is also a U.S. flag and the presidential seal. Inside is the president of the United States.

The plane is none other than Air Force One.

Any U.S. Air Force plane carrying the president is considered Air Force One. But, there are two official versions of the plane. They were **modified** by the U.S. Air Force. The two are rarely seen together. Both are stored in a **hangar**. It is located at Andrews Air Force Base in Camp Springs, Maryland. The base is surrounded by fences. Guards keep watch. High-tech sensors detect intruders.

Air Force One has become one of the most
recognizable symbols of the president.

This particular Air Force One is a custom-made
Boeing 747. It is as tall as a six-story building. The
plane is 232 feet (70 m) long. It has a wingspan
of 195 feet (59 m) and nearly 4,000 square feet
(371 sq m) of interior space. At top speed, the plane
travels from 630 to 700 mph (1,014 to 1,127 kmh). The
plane is a symbol of the U.S. presidency. It is easily
recognizable wherever it flies.

Members of the Air Force 89th Airlift Wing surround President
Barack Obama at Andrews Air Force Base on May 4, 2015.

Air Force One is known as the president's
global command center. It has many great security
features. The plane can withstand a nuclear blast
from the ground. Air Force One's windows are

bulletproof. Each wing has mirrors to confuse **infrared** missiles. Electronic **countermeasure** defense systems jam enemy radars. Hidden flares in the wings can be dropped. These flares can confuse heat-seeking missiles.

Air Force One is operated and maintained by the Air Force's 89th Airlift Wing. This highly skilled group also operates 15 other business jets. Those jets carry members of Congress and the president's Cabinet. About 25 crew members service Air Force One.

The men and women of the 89th Airlift Wing pride themselves on perfection. Their top priority is a flawless mission. That mission is to protect those inside Air Force One.

HOW THE PRESIDENT GETS AROUND

Air Force One is not the president's only official vehicle. Any vehicle carrying the president is given the call sign "One." This helps avoid confusion. A modified helicopter used by the military is code-named Marine One. There is also an armored limousine. It has 5-inch (13 cm) thick bulletproof windows. When the president flies on a commercial airplane, it is called Executive One.

CHAPTER 2

From Horses to Planes

The president of the United States has always needed to travel. Earlier presidents such as George Washington and Thomas Jefferson traveled on horses. But that changed with the rise of railroads.

Railroads spread across the country in the 1830s. Presidents started using them as a primary form of travel in the late 1800s and early 1900s. They campaigned by train. They delivered speeches from the caboose. The Secret Service created a special railcar in 1942. Franklin D. Roosevelt was president then. The railcar was called the Ferdinand Magellan. It had a roof of reinforced steel. It also had armor plating and bulletproof windows.

Roosevelt was also the first president to use an airplane while in office. On January 11, 1943, Roosevelt traveled across the Atlantic Ocean to

President Franklin D. Roosevelt stands behind microphones at the rear of a train on September 26, 1934.

Casablanca, Morocco. It is in North Africa. He met with Winston Churchill and other leaders about World War II.

Things changed after that trip. A plane named Guess Where II was assigned to the president. Roosevelt never flew on it. But his wife, Eleanor, used the plane many times.

President Franklin D. Roosevelt's Sacred Cow plane featured an elevator.

Instead, Roosevelt flew on the Sacred Cow.
It had a radio telephone. It could be used to make
calls over radio waves. The Sacred Cow also had a
sleeping area. Roosevelt used a wheelchair. So the

plane had an elevator for him to use for boarding. Harry S. Truman became president in 1945. He replaced the Sacred Cow in 1947. Truman's plane was called the Independence. Its **nose** was painted like a bald eagle. A room inside seated 24 people.

The modern version of Air Force One was born in 1953. President Dwight D. Eisenhower was in office. That December, he was on a plane named the Columbine II. It was flying over New York City. Air traffic controllers identified the Columbine II as Air Force 8610. Another plane, Eastern Airlines 8610, was also flying over New York at the time. The two planes nearly collided in midair!

The Federal Aviation Administration (FAA) had a solution. It decided any plane carrying the president would have its own call sign. It would not be confused with other planes. The Columbine II became the very first Air Force One.

History has been made aboard different versions of Air Force One. President John F. Kennedy was

It might be known as a football, but this briefcase actually holds key nuclear weapon information for the president's use while flying.

killed in Dallas, Texas, on November 22, 1963. Vice President Lyndon B. Johnson took over as president. For this to happen, Johnson needed to take the presidential oath. This is called a swearing-in ceremony. The rushed ceremony took place on Air Force One. Twenty-eight people were there.

President Kennedy's widow, Jacqueline Kennedy, was on board.

Terrorists attacked the United States on September 11, 2001. The terrorists crashed planes into buildings. President George W. Bush learned of the attacks while visiting a Florida school. He wanted to return to Washington, DC. It was too dangerous. So he spent most of the day on Air Force One. The crew kept the president moving and safe. Air Force One flew so fast that fighter jets providing protection alongside had to ask the plane's pilot to slow down. Air Force One landed that night in Washington, DC. The president was safe.

THE NUCLEAR FOOTBALL

What is "the football"? And why does the president carry it? Every Air Force One flight is considered a military operation. The president arrives at Andrews Air Force Base from the White House. He comes in the Marine One helicopter. The football always arrives with the president. But it has nothing to do with sports. The football is a briefcase. It holds the codes for firing nuclear weapons. A guard watches over the football during flight.

CHAPTER 3

Inside the Flying Fortress

Air Force One has some amazing security tools on the outside. But there are also great features inside. The plane has three **decks**. There are two exits at the front of the plane. The president usually exits on the second, or middle, deck. Each exit has its own staircase. The crew does not rely on the airport to supply steps. This is one less thing to have to worry about.

Air Force One's **cockpit** is on the upper deck. Its dials and buttons are **analog**. They look old compared to the rest of the plane's high-tech features. Sleeping areas for the crew are located just outside the cockpit. Air Force One can easily carry 70 passengers and 26 crew members.

Behind the crew quarters is a communications area. Three radio operators are in charge of the

President George W. Bush rides in the cockpit
of Air Force One on June 13, 2006.

Mission Communications System (MCS). Air Force
One has 85 phones. The MCS provides secure
communication for all of them. There is also video
conferencing. The plane has global **transmission**
and reception power.

Air Force One electronics also include roughly
238 miles (383 km) of wiring. This is twice as much

as a typical 747 model airplane. Heavy shielding protects the wiring from a possible electromagnetic blast.

The president's suite is on the second deck. It sits below the cockpit. The suite has a bedroom, bathroom, and workout area. The suite also includes the commander in chief's personal office.

There is a second office next to the president's. It can double as a medical bay. There is always a doctor onboard. He or she can perform surgeries there if necessary.

Also on the main deck are two **galleys**. Meals are made on the plane. Up to 100 people can be served. There are seats for advisors, media members, and other guests.

FILLING UP

In times of danger, Air Force One might need to fly for a long time. But how is this possible? Most planes need to land to refuel. But Air Force One can refuel midflight. There is a hidden fuel cap in the plane's nose. The fuel cap allows another plane to connect a gas pump to Air Force One's nose without having to land.

Air Force One jacket

presidential seal

phone

guest seating

AIRBORNE OFFICE

In the center of the second deck is the president's conference room. It is one of the biggest rooms on the plane. It is sometimes called "the Situation Room." It acts as an airborne command center in times of emergency. One example of this was the September 11, 2001, terrorist attacks.

Two doors lead to the lower deck. One is at the front of the plane. The other is at the back. The lower deck is used for storage. It is split into

The large tables and conference room areas on Air Force One let the president take care of business while traveling.

two compartments. There is special storage and general storage. The special storage area holds enough food for more than 2,000 meals. The food is stored in pantries and freezers.

The main cargo compartment sits at the back of the plane. The plane has an automated baggage loader. This allows Air Force One crew members to load the plane. This is another way to stop possible trouble. The baggage loader is held in the lower deck. Other items, such as exercise equipment, are also stored there.

Of course, not everything about Air Force One is public knowledge. Many security measures are classified. These include advanced electronic and communications systems.

Air Force One might have a lot of room inside. But all of it is built to keep the president safe.

CHAPTER 4

Flying into the Future

Andrews Air Force Base is Air Force One's home. It stays in a hangar there when it is not in use. That is where more than 100 crew members work on the plane. They work around the clock to make sure the plane is ready to fly. These crew members are highly trained Air Force technicians. Every inch of the airplane is checked. It is waxed and polished by hand. That gives it its shiny look.

The blue-and-white look has become famous. That is thanks to President John F. Kennedy and his wife, Jacqueline. In 1962 they met with designer Raymond Loewy. Together they developed the plane's design.

The president is one of the most important people in the United States. He or she needs to be protected at all times. As technology keeps

The maintenance crew at Andrews Air Force Base prepares
a variety of planes, including Air Force One, for travel.

progressing, so will the features of Air Force One.
The "Flying White House" is a powerful symbol of
the United States. It takes the work of many to make
sure it stays flying high.

GLOSSARY

analog (AN-uh-lawg) A device is considered analog if it uses physical parts to show changing properties, like the hands on a clock. The buttons used to control Air Force One are analog.

cockpit (KAHK-pit) The cockpit is an area in the front of an airplane where the captains sit while flying. The cockpit of Air Force One is located on the top deck.

countermeasure (KOUN-tur-mezh-ur) A countermeasure is an action or device used to prevent something bad from happening. Air Force One features a variety of different countermeasures to protect the president.

decks (DEKS) Decks are the levels of an airplane. Air Force One has three decks.

galleys (GAL-ees) Galleys are the kitchen areas of an airplane. There are two galleys on the main deck of Air Force One.

hangar (HANG-ur) A hangar is an enclosed area in which a plane sits when it is not in use. Air Force One's home is a hangar at Andrews Air Force Base.

infrared (in-fruh-RED) Infrared energy is invisible energy that is often given off by heat. Infrared missiles are often known as heat-seeking missiles.

modified (MAH-duh-fyed) Something is considered modified if it has had changes made to it. The military sometimes uses a modified helicopter called Marine One to transport the president.

nose (NOHZ) The nose is the front tip of an airplane. The nose of President Truman's plane had a bald eagle painted on it.

transmission (trans-MISH-uhn) Transmission is the sending of signals or waves from one location to another. Air Force One has transmission capability so the president can communicate with people around the world.

TO LEARN MORE

IN THE LIBRARY

Mattern, Joanne. *Air Force One*. New York: Children's Press, 2015.

Nagelhout, Ryan. *Air Force One*. New York: Gareth Stevens Publishing, 2015.

Smithsonian Institution. *The Smithsonian Book of Presidential Trivia*. Washington, DC: Smithsonian Press, 2013.

ON THE WEB

Visit our Web site for links about guarding Air Force One: **childsworld.com/links**

Note to Parents, Teachers, and Librarians: We routinely verify our Web links to make sure they are safe and active sites. So encourage your readers to check them out!

INDEX

Andrews Air Force Base, 4, 13, 20

Bush, George W., 13

Churchill, Winston, 9
Columbine II, the, 11
Congress, 7

Eisenhower, Dwight D., 11
Executive One, 7

Federal Aviation Administration (FAA), 11
Ferdinand Magellan, the, 8
"Flying White House, the," 21

Guess Where II, the, 9

Independence, the, 11

Jefferson, Thomas, 8
Johnson, Lyndon B., 12

Kennedy, Jacqueline, 13, 20
Kennedy, John F., 11–13, 20

Loewy, Raymond, 20

Marine One, 7, 13
Mission Communications System (MCS), 15

nuclear football, 13

Presidential Cabinet, 7

Roosevelt, Eleanor, 9
Roosevelt, Franklin D., 8–10

Sacred Cow, the, 10–11
Secret Service, 8
"Situation Room, the," 17

Truman, Harry S., 11

U.S. Air Force, 4, 7, 13, 14, 18, 20

Washington, George, 8
World War II, 9